AUSTERITY

WILL KILL THE ECONOMY!

TIM WATKINS

Waye Forward (Publishing) Ltd

Llanishen

Cardiff

CF14 5FA

www.publishing.wayeforward.com

ISBN-13: 978-1514100004

ISBN-10: 1514100002

ABOUT THE AUTHOR

 Tim Watkins graduated from a Russell Group University with a First Class economics degree in 1990.

Between 1990 and 1997 he worked as a policy researcher with the Welsh Consumer Council where he wrote and published several key policy reports including: *Quality of Life and Quality of Service* – an investigation into the provision of residential care homes for older people - and *In Deep Water* – an investigation into the many problems that followed the North Wales (Towyn) floods of February 1990.

Between 1998 and 2010, Tim Watkins worked for the charity Depression Alliance Cymru, initially as a development worker, and between 2003 and 2010 as its Director. During that time he produced several mental health publications for the charity.

Between 2001 and 2010 Tim Watkins was appointed to sit on several Welsh Government advisory bodies including the Health and Wellbeing Council for Wales, the Burrows-

Greenwell Review of Mental Health Services in Wales and the Expert Panel on Depression.

After 2010, Tim Watkins has authored a range of mental health and wellbeing self-help books and booklets, together with two books about charities and a guide to the digital self-publishing revolution.

Tim Watkins is a founder-director of Waye Forward Ltd, a company established to support those individuals and businesses that have previously been unable to access professional design and publishing services.

A qualified Life Coach, he also provides coaching, mentoring and support to other writers.

CONTENTS

THE HOUSEHOLD ANALOGY   5

MORE TAX IN/LESS SPENDING OUT   13

WHERE DOES MONEY COME FROM?   19

YOU CAN'T PAY WITH WIDGETS   27

WHERE DOES A GOVERNMENT SURPLUS COME FROM?   33

THE OTHER SIDE OF AUSTERITY: FEEDING THE BANKS   41

PEAK PRIVATE DEBT   49

AN ALTERNATIVE THAT MIGHT WORK   61

FOREWORD

When I first studied economics in the unconventional environs of a trade union sponsored course in Newport, South Wales in the mid-1980s, I was given an analogy for the way an economy operates that has stuck with me to this day. Indeed, the importance of the analogy has grown since the mid-1980s because it directly conflicts with the way modern economists and politicians *believe* the economy works. The analogy is this:

> A man goes to watch his local football team play one Saturday. Unfortunately, the opponents in this match are a particularly popular team. As a result, the ground is more packed than usual. Being short of stature, our man would ordinarily stand at the front of the terrace. But this Saturday he is unable to do so, and finds himself in among the crowd and unable to see.
>
> What should he do?
>
> The obvious answer is to find something to stand on. Our man finds an upturned box and stands on it. For him, this makes absolute sense. But what if the result of our man standing on a box serves to obscure the vision of the people behind him? Wouldn't they then

have to get boxes to stand on? And wouldn't other spectators start to notice the advantage of standing on a box? Pretty soon, everyone in the crowd would be stood on a box. The result is that our man would be back to being unable to see once more.

The broad point here is that an individual pursuing his own best interest does *not* necessarily translate into the greater good of society. This, of course, is heresy in a discipline that reveres the "hidden hand" of the free market. Contemporary economics is quite clear on this – the behaviour of an individual (the micro level) translates directly to the economy as a whole (the macro level). If it is good for a spectator at a football match to stand on a box, then it *must* be good for everyone to stand on a box.

If this were simply a matter of football matches and short men, we could move on. But this is a core failing at the heart of contemporary economics that condemns millions of our fellow citizens to poverty and despair. This is because economists and politicians operate the same misguided logic to debt. Since they themselves would seek to pay off their debts, they assume that *everyone*, including governments, should also pay off their debts. And since their *only* means of paying off debt are to work harder and/or spend less, they pursue policies that oblige that *everyone*, including governments, to work more and spend less in the naïve and misguided belief that this will somehow benefit the economy rather than simply leave everyone in the same place that they started, only now having to carry a box around with them.

Cracks are now appearing in the wall of contemporary neoclassical economics. The banking crash of 2008 shook the foundations – although it is a tribute to the construction that despite their inability either to see the crash coming or to explain its cause, the neoclassicals remain in charge. However, as each of their policy prescriptions for saving the economy– quantitative easing, zero percent interest rates, austerity – come to grief, a growing number of us are rethinking economics and politics in order to develop a new narrative. This concise guide to austerity is, in small part, a step on the road to that new narrative.

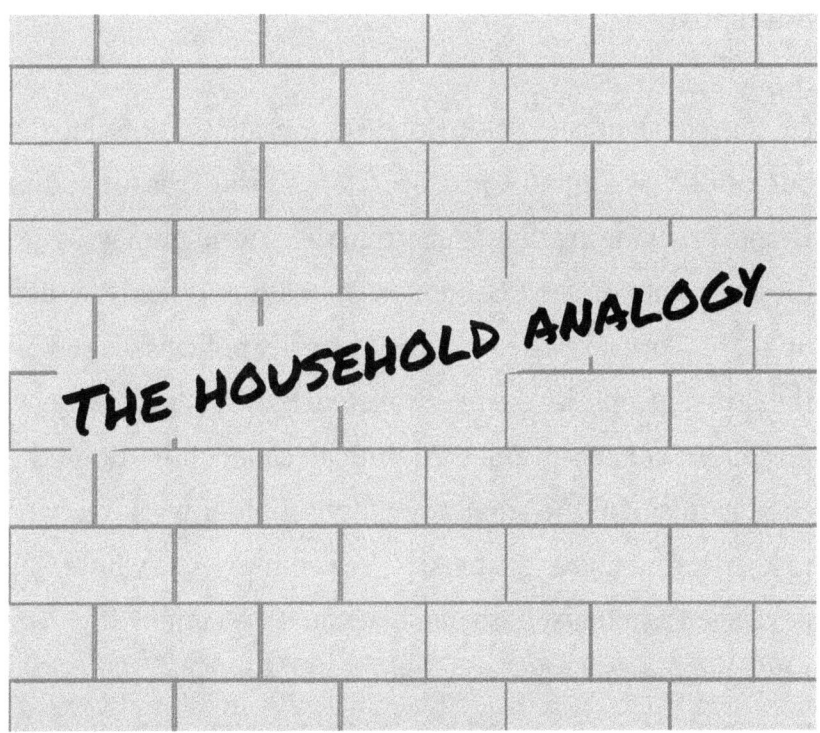

THE HOUSEHOLD ANALOGY

The last government failed to fix the roof when the sun was shining. This was the diagnosis offered by incoming Chancellor George Osborne in 2010. Now, a new government would be forced to take hard decisions that would be all the more painful. And, echoing his ideological mistress, Osborne trotted out TINA – There Is No Alternative.

Of course, Osborne was helped by the idiotic note left by outgoing New Labour Chief Secretary to the Treasury Liam Byrne, proclaiming that "I'm afraid there is no money". And the remnants of New Labour in opposition quickly signed up to the Tory narrative and the austerity policies visited on the British people by the new ConDem coalition government. For public consumption, the political leaders built upon the comely image of the small town householder working hard to keep a roof above his head. The economy as a whole was portrayed as a household just like yours and mine. If you or I borrow too much money, then we face hard choices. We must either take a second job to bring in some more money or we must cut back on our spending. Government, we were told, is exactly the same: "you cannot pay yourself more than you earn".

Because the New Labour government had racked up huge levels of debt between 2008 and 2010, the only options available, they told us, were those that most householders would recognise – earn more money (i.e. stimulate private sector growth in order to increase tax yields) and cut back on outgoings (i.e. cut public spending programmes). According to the new government, fortuitously, cutting public spending would clear the way for the private sector to grow. So this would not be a real hardship. While some people might lose their public sector jobs, these would soon be replaced by private sector employment. So, in the long-term, everyone would benefit.

In practice, the policy has been catastrophic. High-paid, high-skilled jobs have been lost in favour of low-paid, low-skilled jobs that are often part-time or zero-hours. Wages outside the top five percent have stagnated, while the incomes of the most vulnerable – the working poor, the sick and disabled, people with mental illness, together with women who look after disabled children or older relatives – have fallen dramatically. Private sector growth has been anaemic at best; with employment maintained only at the expense of falling productivity – leaving UK companies unable to compete in international markets.

Public services are being hit by the unforeseen consequences of cuts. For example, despite promising to protect the National Health Service, the government has succeeded in creating a series of crises in Accident and Emergency departments as a direct result of the cuts they made to adult social care services, which have removed many of the community-based beds where hospital patients would normally be moved once they were well enough.

For the foreseeable future we can expect even more of the same because both the Tories and the Labour opposition are signed up to the "economy as a household" narrative that dictates austerity as the only road back to prosperity. For the most part, the majority of the 650 members of parliament, adopting this model of the economy is no more than idiocy – they simply do not know any better, and have never bothered to think about the problem. For a handful, however, it is a cynical manipulation designed to dupe the public into accepting an ideological attack on social security and public services. Because, whatever else our increasingly globalized economy is, it most certainly is not a *household*. Even within a household, we might observe that working more and spending less are not the *only* options open to us. We might, for example, consolidate our debts. A household may have access to a credit card deal offering zero percent interest on an existing balance. We could use this to "park" our debt until such time as our circumstances have improved enough to begin paying it off. Government does not need a credit card. It is able to borrow at close to zero percent interest anyway. So, there is actually nothing to stop government from borrowing new loans at zero percent interest in order to pay off debt that currently attracts higher rates of interest.

There is, though, a critically important way in which government is unlike any household you or I have lived in – governments have printing presses. If you or I were to try to solve our difficulties by using a good colour photocopier to print out counterfeit £20 notes, we would end up in jail. This is because since 1844 it has been illegal for anyone *other than the central bank* to print money in the UK. So one thing the government *could* do that a household cannot do is to print new money as an alternative to borrowing it.

Okay, we have heard this line before. Wasn't it Labour Prime Minister James Callaghan back in 1979 who told us that we could no longer print money to spend our way out of recession? In those days, printing new money appeared to cause higher inflation. So – and this is a key reason why the mainstream parties are signed up to austerity – if government today printed more money, wouldn't this simply result in high inflation that would, ultimately, be worse than the privations of austerity?

Although we experience inflation as increasing prices, it is actually a form of currency devaluation. Just as the Roman Emperors devalued their currency by reducing the quantities of gold and silver in the coins, allowing them to mint more, so in the modern world, printing more money without a corresponding growth in the economy can have the same effect – more money chasing the same goods and services leads to price increases. To this, there is an important feedback mechanism – *velocity*. If we expect prices to increase tomorrow, we are more likely to purchase today. So, as inflation takes hold, the velocity (or rate) at which we spend increases. This has a result similar to printing new money called the "multiplier effect". Suppose I earn an extra pound. I might decide to spend it on some flowers for my wife. This means that the florist now has an extra pound. So the florist decides that when she goes for out a meal that evening, she will add the pound to the tip she leaves for the waiter. The extra pound allows the waiter to take a taxi home. The extra taxi fare allows the taxi driver to buy a magazine. And so on. One extra pound is spent over and over, having the effect of growing the amount of money in circulation at any time.

Now, the first thing to say about inflation is it is not necessarily a bad thing. If you are a saver, inflation is a bad thing because you need to secure an interest rate that is at least the same as the rate of inflation just to break even. But in the wider economy, we are better off if savers are encouraged to take risks, as this is the only way of encouraging investment in new (and potentially risky) business ventures. So, inflation can help move investors' money from unproductive asset speculation into productive capital investment. If, on the other hand, you are a borrower, then inflation works for you by cutting the real value of the money you borrow. When people take out mortgages, it is usually the first five years or so that are the most difficult. Having borrowed some multiple of their earnings, they are committed to making that payment every month. However, over time, as inflation increases, their wages increase accordingly. But the monthly payment remains the same. Over time, the mortgage gets easier and easier to pay off. At a global level, the same is true of government debt. As inflation increases, so government finds it easier to pay it off.

In any case, we should be very cautious about making comparisons with the way the *national* economy operated in the 1970s and the way the *global* economy operates today. In this booklet I will make the case that the changes we have witnessed in the past thirty-five years make the comparison entirely unhelpful. These changes have been so profound as to render the currency of today totally different to the money we used in the 1970s. Indeed, one of the key failings of modern politics is the failure to understand this transformation.

In this guide I will argue that in seeking to avoid the ghosts of the 1970s, modern policy makers are creating an even bigger crisis by generating a dangerous deflation in which money is destroyed and spending grinds to a halt. In the face of a massively over-extended banking sector, this process – which is fuelled by austerity economics – threatens to bring the whole economic system crashing to the ground.

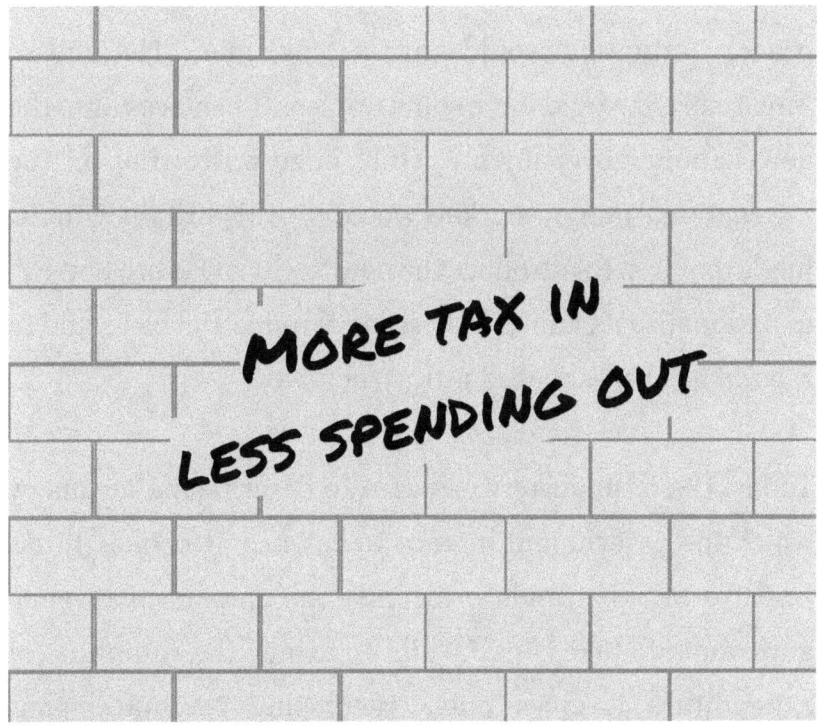

What is austerity?

The term was coined in the aftermath of the Second World War in order to prepare the UK population – still basking in the euphoria of victory – for the privations of a hard-won peace. Rationing would have to continue. The end of American aid would force some unpleasant choices onto the new Labour government. Only huge borrowing on the international money markets would provide Britain with the funds required to introduce the new National Health Service, to nationalise its failing but essential industrial base, and to rebuild its shell-shocked infrastructure.

Today, the term austerity is used to describe the means by which the government intends to balance its books. It has just two broad strands – increase the amount of revenue government takes in, while cutting the amount of expenditure it gives out. Increasing revenue means increasing tax receipts. This must be done in two ways. First, and most obviously, it requires economic growth. The more the economy grows, the more money it generates and thus the more money it has available for taxation. Second, it requires a growth in exports to bring in larger amounts of those currencies that Britain's debt is held in – allowing the debt to be paid off more cheaply.

However, increased tax receipts and export income are unlikely to be sufficient to balance the books. So, in addition, government must cut its spending. Of course, there are political choices here. It is not inevitable, for example, that disability benefits should be cut so that money can be made available for bank bail-outs. Protecting the pensions of the wealthy, while cutting public libraries, is an arbitrary choice. So, understandably this has become the main arena of political debate in modern Britain. All of the main parties are wedded to cuts, but each is prepared to defend its shibboleths.

What is clear from the experience of 2010-15 is that so far, austerity has failed to deliver. The *deficit* – the difference between income and expenditure – has gone down, but it remains a long way from being eliminated. Government debt has risen significantly. In 2010, the coalition government inherited a gross national debt of £0.76 trillion. By 2015, despite austerity cuts, they managed to raise this to £1.36 trillion. The early cuts triggered a recession, and economic growth has been anaemic ever since. Indeed, much of the GDP growth that we have seen has been in the unproductive housing and financial sectors rather than the real economy where people work and firms deliver goods and services. Eighty percent of all new jobs created since 2010 have been in London.

What this suggests is that for austerity to work, government will have to do much *much* more. Simply trying to achieve a surplus on the backs of the unemployed and the disabled is not going to cut it. Some serious tax increases are needed in order to boost revenue, while on the spending side we need to be looking at cutting whole departments rather than tweaking percentages from departmental budgets and hoping for so-called efficiency savings. If the aim – as stated – is to bring the government books into surplus, then we need to be thinking to extremes such as, for example, cutting the entire culture, media and sport budget; taxing pensioners benefits; slashing subsidies to private companies such as the rail operators and the energy generators; and slashing senior management salaries across the public sector. Unfortunately the people and organisations that have sufficient money to pay the kind of taxes that we need are precisely those who have structured their affairs in a way that allows them to escape paying national taxes. Moreover, countries around the world are currently competing with one another to offer the cheapest corporation tax rates in the hope that this will encourage the multinationals to relocate – and hopefully bring new jobs with them. The easiest people to tax are the mass of the middle class PAYE payers who can do little to escape taxes, and upon whose shoulders an increasing tax burden has been piled for several decades.

Cuts have been easy to make thus far because a concerted effort by the government and an increasingly tame BBC – together with the baying cries of the tabloid press – have demonised various outcast groups such as disabled people and immigrants to provide the smokescreen for benefit cuts and slashing local council budgets. However, since it is impossible to balance the books on the backs of the poor, sooner or later, government will have no alternative other than to begin seriously slashing public spending in a manner likely to give rise to the kind of middle class revolt last witnessed when the Thatcher government sought to introduce the Poll Tax in 1990.

If this is not a palatable alternative, then maybe it is time to consider whether austerity is that good an idea. And if it is not, what alternatives are available?

18

We should be seriously concerned to discover that more than ninety-percent of the politicians who have been voting in favour of the austerity programme that is intended to pay off the deficit turn out to have absolutely no idea where money comes from*. Indeed, an alarming seventy percent of MPs believe that the government is the only body that creates money.

One reason why this should alarm us is that paying off the deficit requires actual *money*. And if MPs believe that only government creates money, it is far from clear how they think austerity cuts can work.

The 1970s was the last time Britain operated the kind of printed money system that most of today's MPs believe still operates. The Mint would print new money, which would then be circulated via government departments into the economy. The majority of people were paid in cash. Very few people had bank accounts that allowed them to write cheques† or make direct payments. Similarly, most shops and firms traded solely in cash. Only high-end retailers

* See the Positive Money Campaign – *What does your MP know about money.* http://www.positivemoney.org/2014/08/7-10-mps-dont-know-creates-money-uk/

† Most accounts only allowed depositors to write cheques for cash to be withdrawn at their own bank branch.

offered credit card facilities to the relatively few wealthy people granted the privilege of paying with credit.

Given that most MPs think this is how money operates today, then they must also believe that austerity cannot work. If government is cutting back on the money it spends into the economy, and there is no other source of money, then the amount of money in circulation *must* shrink. This means both that the economy cannot grow and that there will be insufficient money available to pay the additional taxes needed to balance the books. However, while this is proof that most politicians are clueless when it comes to managing the financial affairs of a modern economy (and, incidentally, that PPE degrees* are not worth the paper they are printed on), it does not explain why austerity does not work. This is because politicians are wrong to think that government is the only body that creates money. Indeed, in the modern economy, government is not even the *main* creator of money. In the UK, that distinction goes to just five major banks!

The role of banking within the 1970s system was to provide services that maintained the flow of money through the economy. There would always be a proportion of firms and

* Philosophy, politics and economics degrees are seen as a passport into the mainstream political parties.

households with more money than they wanted to spend. At the same time, there would always be a steady stream of households wanting mortgages and loans, and firms needing capital investment. Banks and building societies operated to bring the two together. They could take in deposits which they would look after on behalf of savers. These savers would enjoy an interest payment as a reward for allowing the bank to lend their savings. Borrowers would enjoy access to investment up front at the cost of making an interest payment back to the bank – and thus the savers – in exchange for the loan. The banks would benefit by charging a relatively small fee – deducted out of the interest payments – to both savers and borrowers.

The system allowed the banks to do more than this. The system of "fractional reserve banking" allowed banks to lend *more money than they had* on deposit, provided that they stayed within strict limits set out by the Bank of England. Based on the observation that it was highly unlikely that savers would all turn up on the same day to ask to withdraw their money, banks could reasonably loan out a multiple of their deposits while continuing to allow for a normal rate of withdrawals from depositors. In this way, a fractional reserve rate of 10:1 would allow a deposit of just £100 could create £990 in loans:

- o   £100 deposited = £10 held and £90 loaned
- o   £90 deposited in the borrower's account = £9 held and £81 loaned on
- o   £81 deposited = £8.10 held and £72.90 loaned
- o   £72.90 deposited = £7.29 held and £65.61 loaned
- o   £65.61 deposited = £6.56 held and £59.05 loaned
- o   £59.05 deposited = £5.91 held and £53.14 loaned
- o   £53.14 deposited = £5.31 held and £47.83 loaned

And so on...

This process gave the central bank considerable power to increase or decrease the amount of money in the economy by varying the fractional reserve rate. If, instead of insisting that the banks keep 10 percent on reserve, the central bank allowed them to keep just 5 percent, then the amount of money in the economy would increase. If, on the other hand, the reserve rate went up to 20 percent, the amount of money in the economy would fall sharply.

By the early 1980s, this system was thought to be holding the economy back. Households and companies struggled to get mortgages and loans, not because they had poor credit ratings, but because banks had reached their reserve limits. People wanted to borrow and banks wanted to lend. But the central bank would not allow it. And this was holding the economy back. After all, with house prices increasing, allowing more home ownership was bound to boost the economy.

By the mid-1980s a whole raft of banking and financial sector regulation had been swept away with the so-called "Big Bang". And although banks and governments maintained the pretence of fractional reserve banking, in practice an entirely new form of banking and finance had been created. In place of a banking sector built to serve the economy, the UK government (along with their counterparts in the USA, Europe and Japan) had ushered in a new system in which the economy (and all the households and firms within it) would be forced to serve the banking and financial sector. This was achieved by effectively turning money creation over to the banks. Since notes and coins were still necessary, the central bank would still have responsibility for arranging for these to be minted. However, as more and more of us were paid directly by electronic transfers into much less regulated bank accounts, our need for notes and coins diminished. Today just three percent of the money in circulation is in the form of notes and coins issued by the government. Ninety-seven percent of the money in circulation is electronic money created by banks.

This has major implications for the economy. Government money comes with few strings. If the central bank messes up and prints too much, we might get inflation. If they print too little, we might get deflation. However, get it more or less right and the money they generate allows us to save and invest, spend and consume. Bank-generated money, by contrast comes with the very big string of *compound interest* attached to it.

In the modern economy ninety-seven percent of the money we depend upon is *borrowed* into existence. When, collectively, households and companies take out loans, banks quite literally *create* new money out of thin air. If, for example, you go into the bank to borrow £10,000 to buy a car, the moment that money enters your account you can spend it. However, there is no corresponding loss of money from a saver's or depositor's account. All that happens is that the bank adds a corresponding amount to the loan as an "asset" on its balance sheet. However, because banks charge interest on all of the loans they make, at any time we – collectively – owe more money than there is money in circulation. This makes the whole monetary system vulnerable to cyclical recessions in which individuals, companies *and banks* have to be allowed to fail in order to allow outstanding bad debt to be written off.

By bailing out the banks and setting historically low interest rates as part of the austerity programme, the government has effectively perpetuated the unsustainable weight of bad private sector debt. This, in turn, acts as an absolute break on economic growth because debt repayment is non-discretionary. That is, people and companies will cut back on almost all discretionary spending before they will default on their debts.

Furthermore, with UK private debt at 175 percent of GDP, there are insufficient new borrowers to generate sufficient new money to pay off the existing debt together with the existing interest. As a result, the entire economy is slowly but surely grinding to a halt as demand falls and deflation sets in.

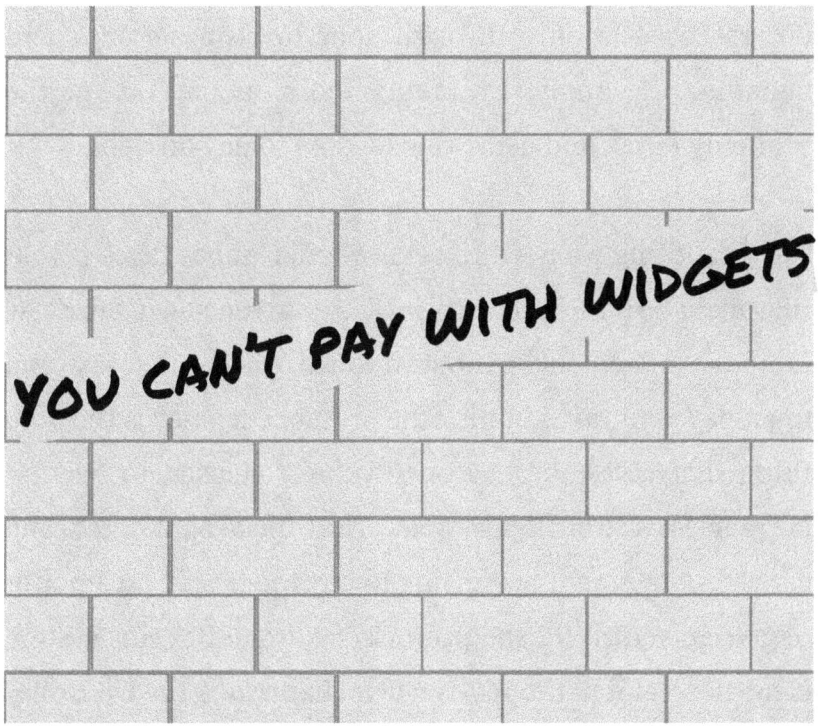

Austerity is – we are told – meant to allow government to balance the books by cutting the amount of money it spends while simultaneously increasing the income it receives through taxation. In essence, this means government is removing money from the economy in two ways. First, by cutting the amount of government-generated money that enters the economy through spending on services and benefits. Secondly, by taking more money out of the economy in tax and using this income to pay off debt.

The first thing we need to acknowledge about taxes is that they *must* be paid in the official state currency – in our case, *Pounds*. Indeed, in the modern world, the law that says you must pay your taxes in the official state currency is the *only* thing that gives the currency value. It used to be that currencies were backed by gold. The official banknotes even carried a statement promising to pay the bearer an amount of gold in return for the promissory note. But this system came to an end in the 1970s when Nixon took the US Dollar off the Gold Standard. By the 1980s all of the major currencies around the world were also free-floating and backed by nothing more than the reputation and standing of the government that issued the currency. However, for the people who live and work *within* the economic area where a currency operates, currency is not free-floating because they are obliged to pay their taxes in just the one national currency. I can have all of the Dollars, Yen and Euros I want, but at the end of the financial year if I don't have enough *Pounds* to pay my taxes, I am in trouble. So, in the UK, we – and the firms we work for – are obliged to do business in Pounds.

So how do we – and the firms we work for – get these Pounds? Well, *we* get Pounds by selling our time to an employer. For most of us this means having a contract of employment in which we are paid an hourly rate in exchange for our working a set time period. A smaller number of us will be self-employed (in which case we have to sell our labour over and over) or will not be guaranteed set hours. Nevertheless, the deal is broadly the same – we work for someone else for a period of time in order to get Pounds.

So where do the firms we work for get the Pounds to pay us? We have already seen that if you print your own Pounds, you end up in jail. The same would happen if firms began to print their own counterfeit money. The firms that we work for pay us to make and sell widgets – the goods and services that power the economy. It is unlawful for firms to try to pay their employees in widgets – although many firms offer discount schemes as an alternative to paying higher wages. The main reason for this is that it is an anti-competitive practice – it gives the firm we work for an advantage over its competitors by, in effect, obliging us to buy from our firm. However, it is also frowned upon by the government because *you cannot pay taxes with widgets.*

So the firms we work for have to find a way of exchanging widgets for Pounds. This is done in the marketplace. And we are so used to engaging in this process of buying and selling that we seldom stop to wonder where all of the money in circulation came from in the first place. So long as the firms we work for continue to sell widgets for Pounds, and so long as we receive some of those Pounds as wages, everyone is happy. Even George Osborne is happy because a percentage of those Pounds return to the government through taxes.

Nevertheless, actual pounds have to come from somewhere. Since ordinary people do not create them, firms do not create them, and government refuses to create them, there is only one other place where pounds can be created – *banks*!

Once you understand this, you begin to glimpse the problem – in our debt-based money system, every pound created is in the form of debt that must be paid off with interest. So there are never enough Pounds in circulation at any time. The only way of obtaining more Pounds is for more households and more firms to borrow more money. But there comes a point where there is so much debt in the system that households and firms want to pay off debts; not borrow more. When this happens, we have a cyclical recession.

All too often, recessions leave firms holding more widgets than there is money to buy them. Unable to exchange widgets for Pounds, firms are obliged to lay off workers. But this results in even fewer Pounds in circulation (as workers become social security recipients – or "scroungers" as the mainstream political parties prefer to view them). This, in turn, means that firms end up with even more widgets than they can sell. So firms lay-off even more workers. And so the downward spiral goes. And all the while, government sees tax receipts fall *because you cannot pay your taxes in widgets.*

The question this raises is, with insufficient money in the system already, how does government increase the income it receives in taxes while simultaneously cutting public spending *and generating economic growth?* To any sensible person – i.e. someone who is neither a politician nor an economist – these actions are entirely contradictory.

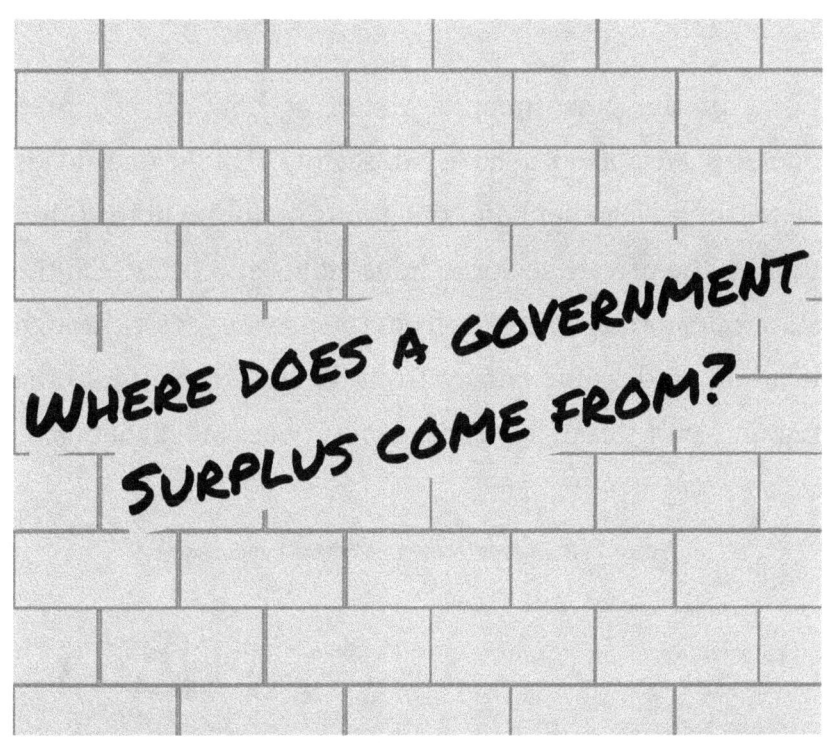

For the government to balance the books, it must receive more currency than it spends. It cannot balance the books with widgets, it must raise **Pounds**. This raises questions about where the money will come from. The stock answer is *economic growth*. We need to unpack this belief in order to see the fallacy behind it.

First, in the government's vision of how an economy operates, we appear to have two sectors. On the one side is state (the government and the public sector). On the other there is the private sector of households and firms. On the state side, money comes in from the private sector through taxation, and money moves from the government into the public sector through spending on services and benefits:

Figure 1: Politicians' Austerity Model of the Economy

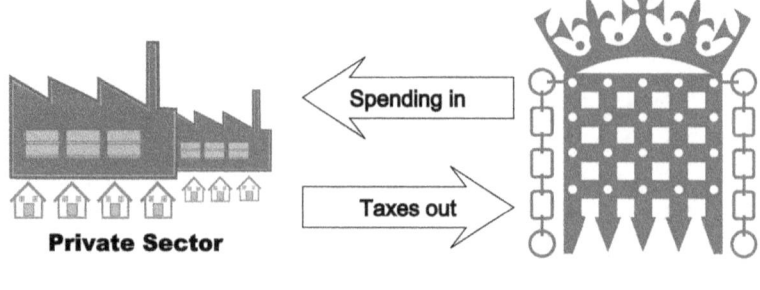

Although government spending initially goes into the public sector to fund public services and social security, these act as a conduit for money to move into the private sector, since recipients of pensions and benefits use the money to purchase private goods and services, while public services procure their supplies from private companies. However, if government operates austerity policies aimed at balancing the books, this requires that it cuts the money it spends into the economy through public services and benefits, while increasing the money it takes from the private sector in taxes:

Figure 2: Austerity Model

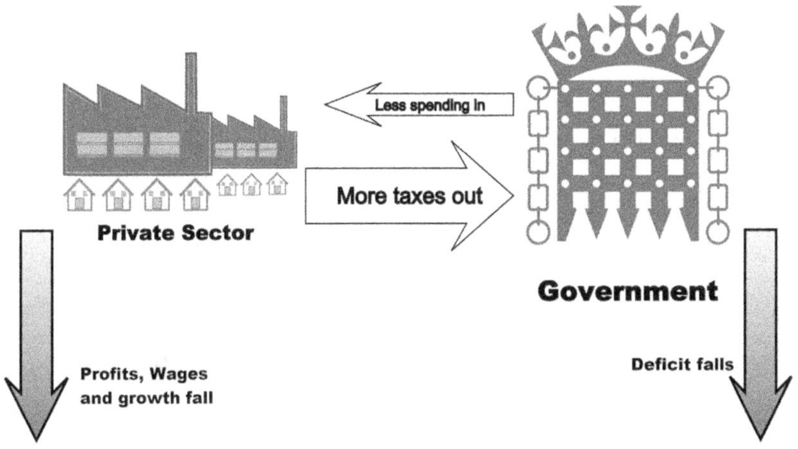

Less spending in

More taxes out

Private Sector

Government

Profits, Wages and growth fall

Deficit falls

By definition, this means that the amount of money available to the private sector *must* shrink, causing recession and deflation... unless the sector can obtain Pounds from another source. For more than three decades, this is where banks came into play. As we have seen, in practice almost all of the money in circulation is loaned into existence by banks:

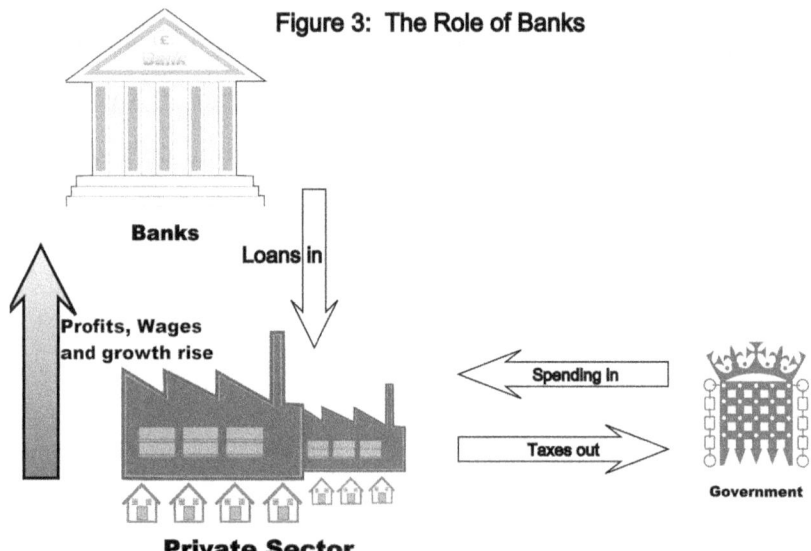

Figure 3: The Role of Banks

Banks invest *new* money in the form of loans into the private sector. This allows firms to purchase new capital and employ new labour. The result is that the economy begins to grow. As the economy grows, there is more money in the private sector, and a proportion of this can be collected in taxes, allowing the government to balance the books. However, while this approach paid dividends in the 1980s and 1990s, when most households were taking out loans for the first time – particularly through the explosion in home ownership – there are problems today because of the already high burden of private debt. Over-extended firms and households are disinclined either to invest or spend any additional money they are able to obtain. Rather, they are inclined to pay off their existing debts first. In these circumstances, austerity policies simply serve to remove even more money from the private sector:

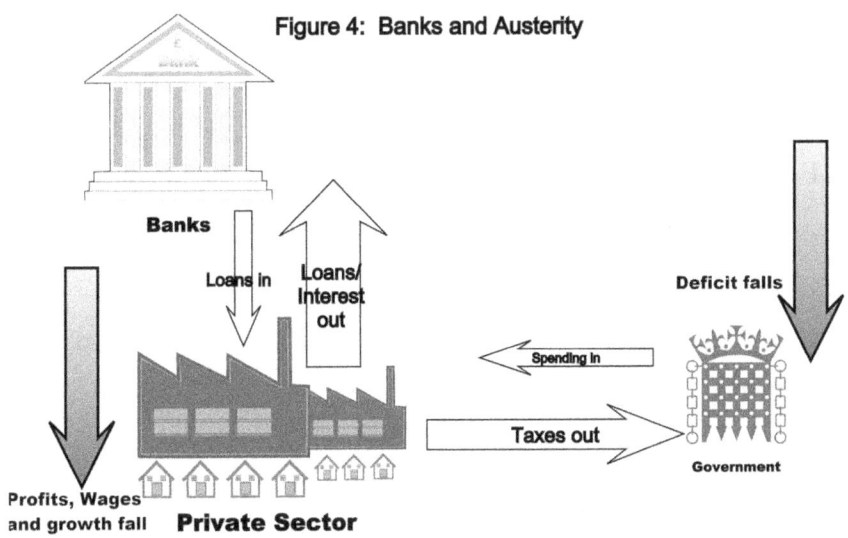

Figure 4: Banks and Austerity

In practice, just as money is created out of thin air when a bank makes a loan, so money disappears into thin air once more when a borrower pays off a loan. Just as nobody loses money when someone takes out a loan, nobody gains money when the loan is paid off. All that occurs is that the "asset" on the bank's balance sheet is cancelled out. So when there is already a high level of private debt in the economy, the private sector tends to destroy money by paying off its debts. This makes absolute sense for individual firms and households, but it has a depressing impact on the economy as a whole.

The only other way the private sector can obtain Pounds is through exports. Just as the UK government holds other countries' currencies, so those other countries hold Pounds. If the UK private sector were able to export significantly more widgets than it imports, this would bring in additional Pounds. However, the UK economy is a net importer of widgets. Moreover, because every other government on earth is attempting to boost exports, they have all devalued their currencies in an attempt to make exports cheap and imports expensive. The result is that even if the UK private sector could become a net exporter, this would not generate sufficient additional Pounds to make a difference.

In the end, the UK government has just two options available. Either it must find a means of encouraging a sufficient proportion of private households and companies to take on massive additional debts or it must reverse the austerity policies. And since you cannot encourage already over-extended firms and households to borrow while you are simultaneously making across the board cuts and seeking to increase taxes, you either ditch austerity or you face the kind of prolonged economic depression that Japan has been going through since 1990.

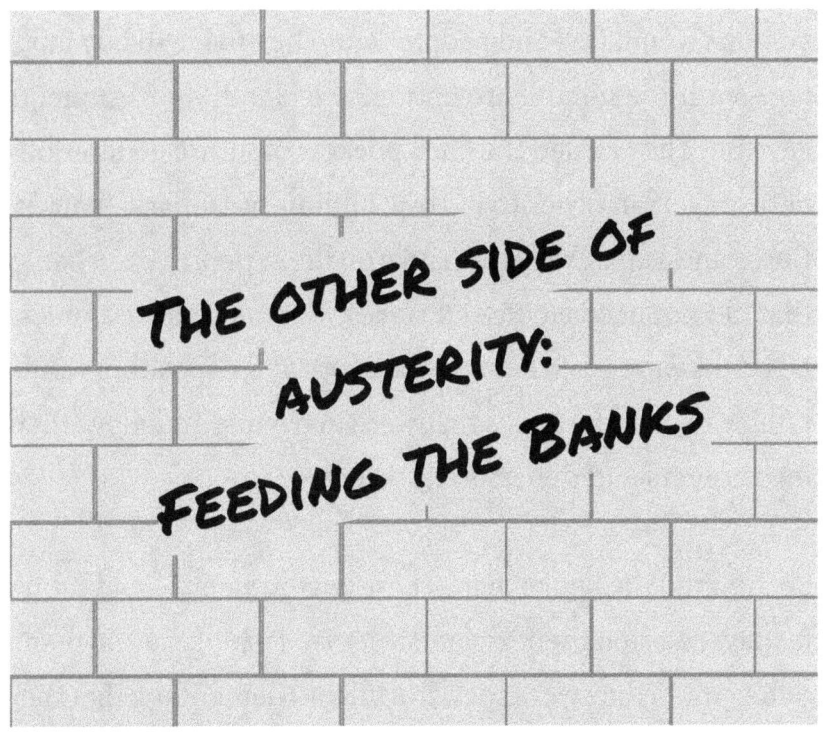

In 2008, the Banks and their apologists went cap in hand (or, more accurately *gun* in hand) to their respective governments and asked them for bail outs. The banks, they claimed, were "too big to fail". Unless radical action was taken, the world economy would be plunged into chaos. Cashpoints would stop dispensing cash, electronic payment systems would fail, and people would be unable to buy food. So – with the notable exception of Iceland – governments gave in. They raided the back pockets of future generations of taxpayers in order to borrow billions of Dollars, Pounds, Euros and Yen to keep the banks on life support. Even banks that did not need a handout were given one, because unless all banks were bailed out, speculators and depositors would be able to spot the banks that were in trouble and move their investments and deposits elsewhere.

So, how did the banks thank these governments – and future taxpayers – for their generosity? By lashing out at them, telling them they were spendthrift, and demanding that they rein-in public spending in order to balance the books! This attitude should have been enough to convince the public that never again should we bail out banks or any other failing corporations. Because without moral hazard – having to face the consequences of bad decisions – you not only place corporations above the free market, but you end up placing them above the law*.

In fact, far from curbing public handouts to the banks, the whole austerity programme is underwritten by huge ongoing public subsidies in the form of zero percent interest rates, depositor insurance, quantitative easing and *Help to Buy* schemes.

Although the first of these has been sold as being a means of saving heavily indebted households and companies from collapse, even this is primarily a subsidy to the banks. This is because any increase in interest rates will result in large scale defaults on private debts. And in these circumstances, companies and households will be declared insolvent and banks will not get their money back. However, the zero percent interest policy has a much more insidious consequence for the economy – it removes risk from lending and investment decisions. The historical justification for charging interest on a loan – a practice condemned by the major religions as *usury* – is that investment comes with risk. For example, a bank may make loans to 10 start-up businesses, but only five of them will succeed. But by

---

* Despite a trail of fraud and corruption by UK-based banks that includes laundering money for terrorist organisations and drug cartels, not a single banker has been brought to court, let alone sent to jail.

charging interest on the loans, the bank can at least offset some of the risk. If, however, the banks themselves can borrow money at zero percent interest, but then charge much higher rates of interest to borrowers, there is no risk at all. Indeed, many banks have ceased lending money to companies and households, preferring instead to use the free money they receive from the central bank to directly buy up speculative assets such as houses, shares and even fine art. So long as these asset bubbles continue to rise at a much greater rate than inflation, the banks are guaranteed to make money. Of course, all asset bubbles burst eventually.

Where banks do lend into the private sector, they tend to be risk-averse. Money is available for property purchases, where the loan can be made against an asset which the bank can repossess if things go wrong. This further pumping up of the new housing bubble has also been aided by government schemes that underwrite some of the "risk" in providing mortgages to first time buyers. Loans are much harder to come by for businesses seeking investment in new ventures where there are no assets to use as security against the loan – even though, ultimately, it is only investment in these kinds of venture that will deliver the economic growth that will revive our flagging economy.

Quantitative easing has similarly failed to deliver. Quantitative easing is almost the reverse of the process by which governments borrow money. When governments want to borrow money, they auction bonds, which are bought by the banks. In contrast, through quantitative easing, the central bank uses new central bank reserves that are simply printed out of thin air to buy back government bonds and other assets that the banks were holding. This allows government to claim that they are not "printing money", because when the emergency is over, they will be able to sell these bonds and assets back to the banks. But this is a mere fig leaf, since any attempt to sell these bonds back will result in a crash in their price, preventing the central bank from ever getting its (i.e. *our*) money back.

The idea behind quantitative easing was that government money, pumped into the banks, would be loaned out into the private economy. As more households and firms borrowed, so more new money would enter the system. This, in turn, would create the conditions for economic growth. But, only a tiny fraction* of the quantitative easing money given to the banks has trickled out into the productive economy. The vast bulk has been used for asset speculation and share buy-backs (in which banks keep their share price artificially high by purchasing their own shares).

* The Positive Money Campaign puts it at about 8p in every £1.00

In many parts of the UK today, people's houses are "earning" more than the people themselves can ever dream of earning. However, as with all asset bubbles, the price increase is an illusion. Most people buy houses to live in, not as an investment to be sold when the price is right. And in the end, only one person gets to sell at the highest price. Once an asset bubble reaches the point at which more people want to sell than buy, the result is *always* a crash. As the old Wall Street saying goes, "asset bubbles climb up the staircase and fall down the lift shaft." When the UK's current housing bubble collapses, it will be sudden and ruinous.

Not all of the fault for this state of affairs can be laid at the feet of the banks. Because economists and politicians have little grasp of how banks operate, they have deluded themselves into believing that private debt has no impact on the wider economy.

> "It may astonish non-economists to learn that conventionally trained economists ignore the role of credit and private debt in the economy – and frankly, it is astonishing. But it is the truth. Even today, only a handful of the most rebellious of mainstream 'neoclassical' economists – people like Joe Stiglitz and Paul Krugman – pay any attention to the role of

private debt in the economy, and even they do so from the perspective of an economic theory in which money and debt play no intrinsic role. An economic theory that ignores the role of money and debt in a market economy cannot possibly make sense of the complex, monetary, credit-based economy in which we live. Yet that is the theory that has dominated economics for the last half-century."*

University economics courses continue to teach the fiction that banks merely operate as middlemen between "patient savers" and "impatient borrowers". That is, they think that if a borrower is given a £10,000 loan that somewhere in the system a saver's account has had £10,000 removed from it. If this were true, then the only consequence of lending would be that purchasing power would be transferred from one part of the economy (savers) to another (borrowers). However, this is a fiction:

> "In the modern economy, most money takes the form of bank deposits. But how those bank deposits are created is often misunderstood: the principal way is through commercial banks making loans. **Whenever a bank makes a loan, it**

* Keen, S. 2011. *Debinking Economics – the naked emperor dethroned?* (revised and expanded edition). p6

simultaneously creates a matching deposit in the borrower's bank account, thereby creating new money."***

When banks make loans, they generate entirely new money. And as a consequence they generate indebtedness that can only be overcome by exponentially increasing the amount of debt in the system. Unless this can be done, the economy will slow, and there will be insufficient money in the system to pay the debt *and the interest*.

* Michael McLeay, Amar Radia and Ryland Thomas. *Money creation in the modern economy.* Bank of England Quarterly Bulletin 2014.

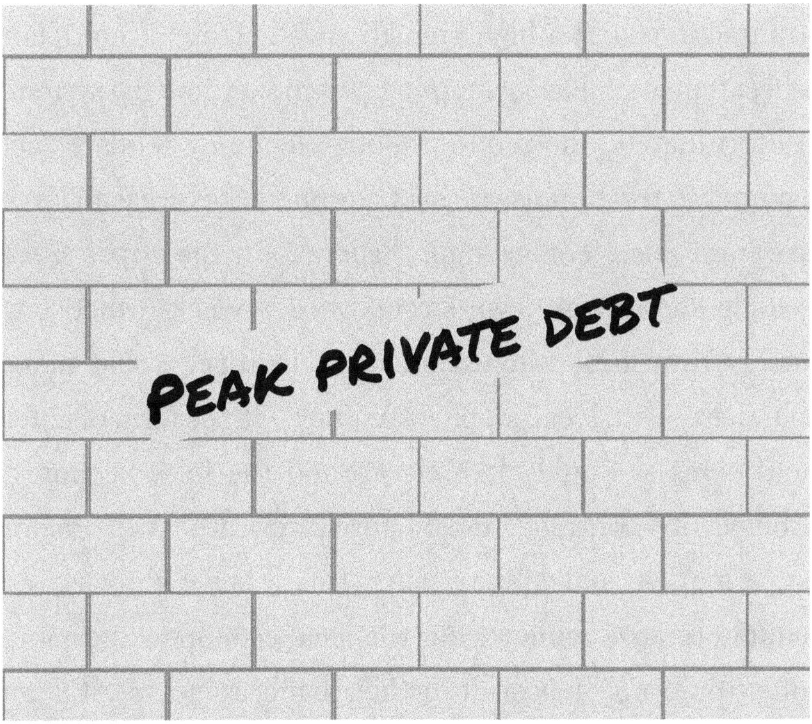
PEAK PRIVATE DEBT

In a debt-based monetary system, there are only two ways of paying off the loans *and* the interest on them. The less obvious method is to increase the velocity of money. This involves two elements – the number of transactions that money is used for *before* it ends up back at the bank; and the speed at which these transactions occur. Enough transactions and a high enough speed create a multiplier effect that is similar to pumping new money into the system. Unfortunately, the modern global economy tends to act counter to this because most of our purchases are with large corporations. For example, whereas in the 1970s most people shopped in local stores whose owners would buy stock from local wholesalers who, in turn, would make purchases with local suppliers, money – in the form of notes and coins – would circulate around the local economy. Today, in contrast, most purchases are with major supermarkets and online retailers (many based abroad) who simply remove money from the local economy, and more often than not deposit it at their bank, removing it from circulation. Moreover, pumping money into asset bubbles – such as the current UK housing market – has a similar effect, by creating household debt that is non-discretionary (default and you lose your home). Households with high levels of debt do not have much (or any) discretionary income to spend in the productive economy; most or all of their income is non-discretionary, going to pay for food and fuel *and* to service and pay off debts.

Given that the current configuration of the global economy works against increasing the velocity of money – a situation that has been worsening for the last three decades – there is only one other means of generating sufficient new money to pay off both existing loans and interest: that is to take out even more loans. And because interest comes at a percentage over time, the growth in borrowing must happen in a particular way... it must grow *exponentially*.

The mathematician Dr Albert Bartlett warned that the failure to understand the exponential function is humanity's greatest weakness. This is because exponential growth involves a doubling of whatever is growing over a period of time. And while this appears manageable with small quantities, growth gets spectacular when the numbers get big.

There is a famous story about the invention of the game of chess that illustrates this point. Apparently, the King of Persia was so impressed with the game that he offered its inventor any reward he chose to name. The inventor asked only that the king place a single grain of rice on the first square of the chessboard and then double up on each of the remaining 63 squares. So the King sent a servant to get sacks of rice from the store house. However, very quickly the King found that there was not enough rice in the kingdom (or, indeed, the world) to pay the reward:

- Row one: 1; 2; 4; 8; 16; 32; 64; 128
- Row two: 256; 512; 1,024; 2,048; 4,096; 8,192; 16,384; 32,768
- Row three: 65,536; 131,072; 262,144; 524,288; 1,048,576; 2,097,152; 4,194,304; 8,388,608
- By the end of row four, this had grown to 2,147,483,648.
- By the end of row six: 549,755,813,888.
- By the end of row six: 140,737,488,355,328.
- By the end row seven: 36,028,797,018,964,000.
- By the end of row eight: 9,223,372,036,854,780,000 – more grains of rice than existed on Earth!

If we were to draw these figures on a graph, it would look like this:

For much of the time nothing seems to be happening. Then, right at the end there is a sudden and massive increase. Remember that the *rate of growth* is constant. What makes the difference is that at a certain stage the numbers involved get big enough to allow a massive increase. This point is known to mathematicians as the "hockey stick", and it can be found in all kinds of human activity.

Human population growth across the millennia since our ancestors first discovered agriculture looks very similar. For most of human history, nothing much seemed to be happening. Then, from the eighteenth century things really started to take off. By 1960 the population had reached 3 billion and today – just 55 years later it has more than doubled to pass 7 billion!

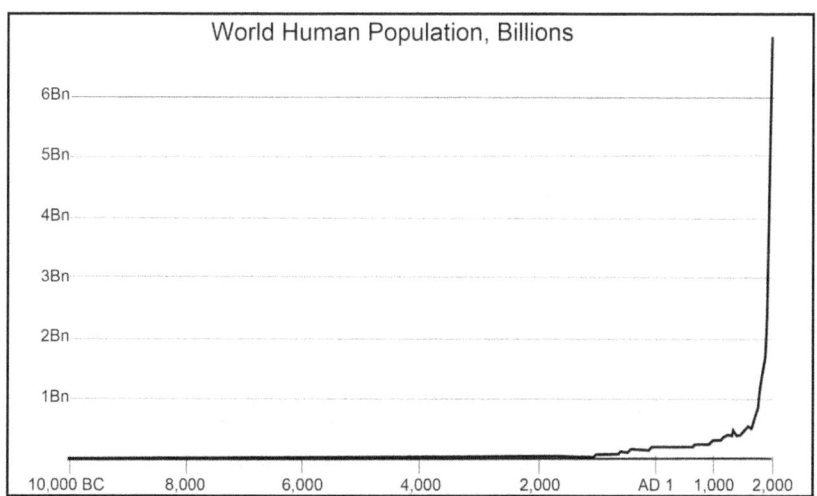

So what does this have to do with money, debt and austerity? Well, our money supply and our economy must also grow *exponentially*. And it turns out that even a modest rate of growth – let's say 3 percent – can have a dramatic impact because another way of stating a rate of growth of *just* 3 percent is "a doubling every 23 years". That is, if we intend growing the economy at 3 percent, what we are saying is that we want to be using double the resources, double the energy, double the capital and double the labour in just 23 years' time. On a finite planet, where we are running into barriers, whether we can keep doing this is questionable.

These limits are also appearing in our debt-based money system:

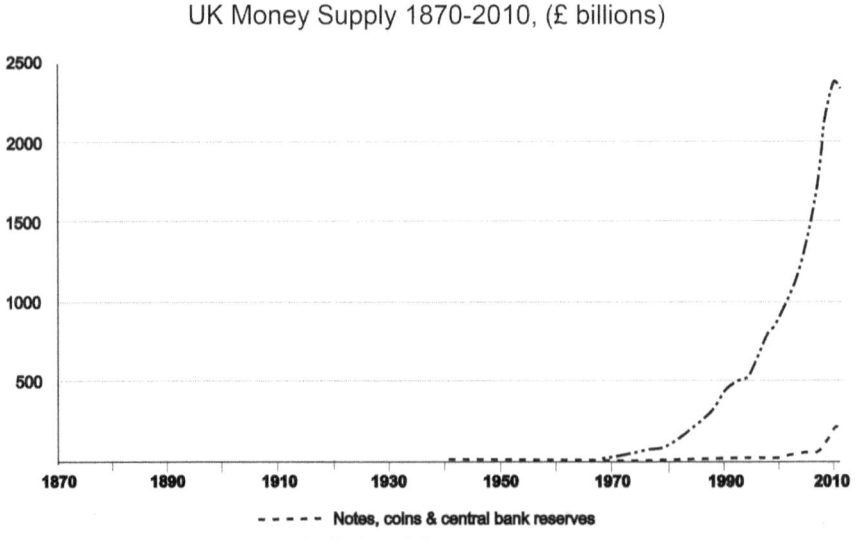

UK Money Supply 1870-2010, (£ billions)

- - - - Notes, coins & central bank reserves
.. —... —. Bank-created money

We have witnessed the same process of exponential growth in debt-based money since currencies ceased being tied to the Gold Standard in the early 1970s. If we are to pay back the debt and the interest, we will need to double rapidly the amount of debt-based money in circulation. But this raises an important question about limits. There are only so many things that private households and companies can borrow money to buy... and most of them have already been bought! Companies may invest in new premises and equipment. However, most of the really big – and thus expensive – factories, datacentres and call centres have been moved offshore to countries that have less regulation, lower wages and fewer pollution controls. Compare Britain's biggest factory – the Nissan plant in Sunderland with its 6,000 employees – with the giant Foxconn plant in China with its 190,000 employees and you begin to see the limits on British private company borrowing.

Private households are also reaching limits. Houses are by far the most expensive item private households buy. However, in the face of a massive housing shortage, the housing bubble is the only thing maintaining high borrowing. But high prices work to exclude many households from the housing ladder, so they cannot be a long-term alternative to building enough houses.

Almost all of the people who are currently considered credit worthy already have houses. When people in this category move, they seldom require mortgages for the full cost of their next house; only for the difference between the price of their new house and the income from the sale on their previous house. So this group simply cannot borrow sufficient new money into the system.

Beyond houses, the next most expensive items are vehicles and student loans. However, these are an order of magnitude less in price than housing. In order to borrow sufficient new money into the system, we would need almost everyone considered credit worthy to buy a new car *and* start a three year degree course. This, of course, is not going to happen. It takes around 25 years to replace the British car fleet because the majority of households buy second hand cars – often those bought new by companies. Moreover, these second hand cars often get sold on several times before ending up at the scrap yard. So the majority of borrowing for cars is relatively small scale and far too little to borrow sufficient new money into the economy. Nor can student loans save the day simply because anyone with an income sufficiently high to be able to afford to pay off a student loan already has a better job than they could hope to get if they were to give it up to return to education. This tends to restrict new student loans to school leavers wishing to remain in higher education. And there are not enough of these to borrow into existence the money that the economy needs.

Beyond these big ticket items come all of the home improvements, white goods and household electronics that households borrow for. These seldom involve more than £1,000 at a time, and cannot hope to generate sufficient new debt-based money to allow the economy to grow at that modest rate of three percent per year – that is, to double in size by 2038.

There is also a demographic problem facing the British economy. There are lots of people at the economically unproductive ends of the population – the young and the old – but far too few in the productive middle groups aged 20 to 40 – those who would be most likely to take on significant new debt. The largest population group is aged 40 to 50, a group much less likely to take on new debt. The young (16 to 20) are a problem because on the one hand they do not borrow for the kind of high-value items – houses, cars, and home improvements – that are required for economic growth; and on the other hand, young workers' wages are being squeezed, making them far less credit worthy. Indeed, the main borrowing in this age group is in the form of student loans that work to make this group even *less* credit worthy as they enter middle age. The old are a problem for a different reason – for the most part, they have already bought the various items that the economy needs people to borrow for. Older people spend on average £25,000 less per year than middle aged people simply because there are few things beyond their day-to-day needs that they do not already have. Moreover, once past retirement age, older people struggle to secure large loans from the banks – so what they have not already bought, they are unlikely ever to buy.

So the future of the debt-based money system *must* depend upon a shrinking middle aged population. But this group is being squeezed from several directions. Most notably, this group is facing the biggest hit from austerity policies that on the one hand cuts the public services they rely upon – often forcing them to make private arrangements – and on the other hand they are being asked to shoulder a greater proportion of the tax burden as government seeks additional money to cut the deficit. This leaves the one group within the population with both the potential means and the potential desire to borrow in practice much less able to do so.

As Ronald M. Laszewski* puts it:

> "The primary implication of our analysis remains and is re-enforced: there appears to be no way to avoid the dire economic consequences of an over-accumulation of personal debt."

There is, apparently, no way out.

* Laszewski, M. *Peak Debt.* July 2008. P13.

AN ALTERNATIVE THAT MIGHT WORK

It is doubtful that we can save the modern, debt-based global economy from itself. Our political leaders and the economists who advise them are all schooled in the neoclassical economics model that created the crisis in the first place. Their solution? More of the same! More bank-created money... more private sector debt... more asset bubbles... more crashes and crises for the future.

Less obviously, but much more worryingly, almost all of the economics departments of universities around the world, together with the academic economics journals have excluded all opposition more effectively than the North Korean Politbureau. Over time, as economists who offered an alternative perspective retired, they were replaced by neoclassical clones. The result is an environment about as open to alternative views as the Spanish Inquisition. In academia if you are not a neoclassical economist (with a few notable exceptions) you do not get work and you most certainly do not get published. The result is that the handful of economists who predicted and explained the 2008 crash and its consequences have been effectively side-lined. Meanwhile, mainstream economists continue to cheer-lead austerity policies that can only result in an even more devastating crash in future.

So the most likely future facing us is one in which governments undermine their national economies by massively cutting the amount of money in circulation. This will provide the real economic basis for the sudden collapse of the asset bubbles that the banks have blown up in housing, US shale oil, shares, government bonds and even fine art. The only question this time around is whether further bank bailouts will be politically possible... and even if they are, have the "too big to fail" banks become too big to *save*?

It will probably take another crisis to change direction. Even then, there is no guarantee that we will finally reform the system. Only when we acknowledge that the single biggest threat to the economy is the massive level of bank-generated private sector debt – itself the inevitable consequence of allowing banks to print money – can we hope to come up with a solution.

Throughout history only one workable solution to the over accumulation of private debt has ever been found – *debt write off*. Whether this occurs through a debt jubilee, in which all outstanding debt is written off and the system re-set, or – most probably – through mass defaults and bankruptcy, the outcome is always the same – unsustainable and unrepayable private debt disappears into the ether (from whence it should never have been allowed to come in the first place).

In the modern world this has serious implications because, although much of the problem has been caused by reckless lending by banks, egged on by reckless politicians wanting the benefits of economic growth without the hard work that this implies, the fact is that much of the money that would have to be written off is people's pension funds, savings, insurances and other benefits. Simply writing off debt could cause considerable harm to people on very modest incomes who rely on their savings to maintain their standard of living. This, indeed, is one of the arguments that the proponents of austerity will make to justify their misguided attempts to "balance the books". However, in practice austerity will create the very defaults and mass bankruptcies that its proponents claim to want to prevent.

Fortunately there is no need to simply write off debt. There is another way. This is to go back to the one thing that distinguishes a government from a household when it comes to balancing the books. If you or I had a money printing press, we would balance our books by printing enough money to pay off our debts.

So why doesn't government use its "printing press" to pay off its – and more importantly the unsustainable private sector – debts? The answer is twofold. First, there is a misplaced morality in government not doing so. Most of us believe that borrowers should "do the responsible thing" and pay their debts. However, as we have seen, the system is deliberately rigged against borrowers. There was never enough money in the system to pay the debts and the interest. Indeed, the very fact that the banks created the money they lent out of thin air would imply that what we have here is the *sin of usury* in exactly the form that religions around the world throughout the ages warned us never to adopt – everyone in this game has acted immorally!

Second, and more persuasively, there is a fear based on the experience of the 1970s, that printing money will cause inflation. The fallacy here is exposed precisely because the banks have been printing money out of thin air without creating (unmanageable) inflation for more than three decades. Indeed, the operation of the global economy is highly *deflationary* because it has removed the wage and resources pressures that characterised the 1970s. By allowing production to be moved to countries with the cheapest labour force, and by driving down input costs, the global economy prevents the kind of wage-price spiral that helped cause the 25 percent inflation rates of the mid-1970s in the UK... and the global economy would continue to do this in the event of government creating money instead of banks.

What any *sovereign* government* can do is what has been called "unconventional quantitative easing" or more colloquially, a "helicopter drop". In practice, the Bank of England can simply "print" the electronic money that we all see in our bank accounts. It could print sufficient new money to bring private sector debt down to safe levels, and distribute it equally among all adults in the UK population – with this essential proviso: if you are in debt, you *must* use the money to pay off your debt; otherwise, you *must* spend the money on goods and services. The money used to pay off debt does not cause inflation because it immediately disappears out of the system as it cancels debt. Only the money which is spent is inflationary. But this is not necessarily a bad thing, since the impact of austerity has been a trend toward deflation. This would be cancelled out by new money entering the private sector.

By wiping out private debt, unconventional quantitative easing recreates people's discretionary spending. It means that a greater proportion of incomes can be used for

---

* This is why comparisons with Greece are also unhelpful, since Eurozone countries have given up their sovereign ability to create money.

purchasing goods and services rather than merely servicing debt. So on both the written off debt side and the additional spending side; the outcome is a spur to renewed economic growth. In fact, it is theoretically possible to pay back all of the debt *and the interest* created by the banks. This is because a high velocity of money can create a multiplier effect that makes it *appear* that there is much more money circulating through the economy than is actually the case at any one time. But – and this is a huge *but* – this can only work if all of the bank-generated money borrowed into existence is spent in the real, productive economy. That is, it is used by companies to invest in new production and by households to buy goods and services that add value*. What cannot be allowed is the creation of yet more unproductive asset bubbles such as those in housing, shares, government bonds, shale drilling and fine art.

This implies the reinstatement of the type of controls and regulation of the banking industry brought in after the Great Depression, and so frivolously tossed aside by the neoclassical economists and globalists in the 1980s and 1990s. In short, if we are to allow the banks the privilege of being the only bodies in society other than the central bank to create money, they have a responsibility to the public –

* At present less than 20 percent of bank-generated money is loaned for investment in private companies. More than 80 percent is used to finance unproductive asset bubbles.

who, after all, end up picking up the tab when things go wrong – to ensure that the money they create has a public benefit. The alternative is to remove from the banks the privilege of being able to create money.

As long ago as 1844, following an earlier banking crisis in which the UK government had to borrow £2,000,000 in gold from France in order to bail out the banks, Parliament passed the Bank Charter Act to make it illegal for anyone other than the central bank to create money. But this Act did not prevent banks making loans. Nor did it anticipate the development of computers and modern communications networks which have allowed the banking sector to effectively hijack the money supply. There is a good legal argument to say that the last time Parliament voted on the issue, it was their clear intent that banks should be forbidden to create money. And since Parliament has not voted on the issue since, our presumption should be that bank-generated money is unlawfully generated money.

Exactly how money would be generated without banks is not fully clear. Certainly the monopoly on creating electronic money would have to pass to the Bank of England to sit alongside its monopoly on creating notes and coins. However, a political process would have to be developed to determine how much money should be generated at any time. Moreover, this would have to be independent of the day-to-day politics of the UK, because of the temptation for politicians to print too much – inflationary – money in order to fund the reckless promises they tend to make in the run up to elections*.

In addition to this democratising of the national currency, there is good reason to consider developing parallel local currencies such as the Bristol Pound† which are designed to keep spending power circulating within local economies. Indeed, in the city of Bristol, residents are now able to pay their Council Tax in Bristol Pounds, helping to make that local currency even more attractive to local businesses and consumers. Crypto currencies may also have a role to play in future, as they are similar to a gold-backed currency. Because of the way cryptocurrencies like *Bitcoin* are "mined", it is impossible for anyone to create new money out of thin air. Cryptocurrencies are also transparent, as the "block chain" technology behind them ensures that new currency cannot be fraudulently introduced.

---

* The Positive Money campaign are developing this model, and have recently succeeded in getting Parliament to debate the issue. http://www.positivemoney.org

† http://bristolpound.org

Whichever direction we go in, if we are to avoid a future catastrophic collapse of the global economy, the banking industry itself must be restructured to separate retail banking from investment banking in order to protect the current accounts of ordinary depositors. This is because we have developed an economic and civil system that *requires* citizens to have bank accounts. Even the very poorest among us are required to have a "basic bank account" in order to receive benefits and make electronic payments. It is impossible to resister as self-employed or to open a company without a bank account. It is also getting much harder to pay tax, council tax and utility bills without a bank account. However, as we saw in 2008, this captive population of people who have no real choice but to have their money in a bank discovered that the small print in the terms and conditions allowed that any money deposited in a bank *is the property of the bank*!* That is, in the event of the bank running into trouble, depositors have no right to their money. In 2008, depositors faced ruin because the banks had used their deposits to underwrite their risky commercial trading in sub-prime mortgages and collateralised debt obligations. For the most part, the public are indifferent to

* At present, the UK government underwrites deposits up to £85,000. However, it is far from clear how quickly depositors would be able to claim this money in the event of another banking crash.

the fate of commercial banks whose risky investment practices result in bankruptcy. However, when the same banks threaten to take out the high street banking system that we all depend upon for our day to day economic activity, the public ends up having to bail out banks and underwrite current accounts and ordinary savings.

This situation amounts to little more than blackmail by the banks, and it cannot be allowed to continue. In practice this means the complete separation (i.e. something more than the so-called "firewalls" that have been introduced since 2008) of the high street and commercial banking sectors. High street banking – underwritten by public guarantees – would continue to provide the ordinary bank services that we rely upon. Because of the government guarantees, it would allow a safe haven for cautious savers who would earn a small amount of interest on their deposits.

It would also make sense to re-introduce the building society/mortgage lending system that worked to prevent asset speculation in housing. In a country whose economy is undermined by a severe housing crisis, it makes little sense to allow money that should be invested in the real economy to be diverted into property asset speculation that serves only to drive up the cost of housing, the cost of living, and ultimately the cost of employment.

More adventurous savers and investors would be able to make deposits in the exclusively commercial banks. They would receive higher rates of interest because of the higher degree of risk involved and because, free from government support, these banks would be allowed to fail if their investment decisions were to go wrong. Freed from a government safety net that effectively protects banks from the consequences of their reckless investment decisions, shareholders and managers in this sector would have a much greater incentive to *earn* their bonuses by providing proper oversight.

These potential solutions to the predicament we find ourselves in are beginning to enter the mainstream. However, the overwhelming majority of economists and politicians – those who still have no idea what caused the crash of 2008 – continue to believe that private sector debt does not matter, and that the role of government in a depression should be to pay off its own debt. It is likely that we will have to go through an even bigger banking collapse than the 2008 crash before austerity policies finally come to be seen as the nonsense they are.

Until that time, politicians will continue to feed us the illiterate drivel that economies are the same as households.

And since for most of us, household economies are the only ones we have ever had to understand, we will continue to endorse policies that will ultimately destroy our way of life simply because we know no better.

POSTSCRIPT

I take the view that we will only change course *after* the next banking crisis has occurred. Any dispassionate examination of the policies and practices of the main parties of government in the UK* shows that they lack any insight into the nature of the problem that they face, let alone the long-term strategic vision to develop solutions. Indeed, beyond encouraging even more private borrowing to pump up the housing bubble once more, there appears to be no coherent policy at all.

Today there are looming crises that may put rescuing the banking system beyond us. Climate change is already having major impacts on the world economy. Droughts in the grain growing regions of the USA and Russia have already raised concerns about famine, with some commentators anticipating mass hunger in parts of the world by 2020. Underlying this is the unsustainable growth of the human population, which is expected to rise above 9 billion by mid-century. We have many more mouths to feed, but no food to feed them with. In addition, sea level rise threatens to destroy or disrupt 85 percent of the world's cities.

* If anything, the politics of the USA, EU and Japan are even worse.

However, climate change is still a long way off, and may just be the final curtain for the global economy. Much more urgent is a growing energy and resource crisis. This is driven by three forces:

o Geology – there is simply less cheap and easy coal, oil and gas left in the ground for us to use; what is left is going to get expensive

o Development – newly emerging economies (most notably India and China) have developed an insatiable demand for the Earth's remaining supplies of resources and energy. For example, if China were to continue developing at 7.5 percent per year, it would have to be consuming more than 90 percent of the world's coal and 80 percent of the world's oil by 2050.

o Shortage – resource rich countries are increasingly reliant on the resources that they have traditionally exported to fuel their own domestic growth. As demand grows, they will seek to hang on to more of these resources. Since this will drive up prices on global markets for what remains, they will be able to do this while maintaining their income from exports.

This is a particular problem for the UK economy because our early industrial revolution allowed us to consume our best resources centuries ago. Our most recent source of riches – North Sea oil – peaked in 1999, and production has been falling ever since. We now depend on imported oil and gas from some of the most dangerous regions on Earth. And while the UK now generates 15 percent of its energy from renewables and nuclear, this will not be sufficient in the event of disruption in global supply. Without energy – or, indeed, with only intermittent energy – the UK economy will stall.

In fact, dealing with the inherent instability in the banking and finance system is probably the easiest of the problems we face. However, we will not act until it is too late. This is because:

o We are psychologically here/now orientated – we are concerned with ourselves and our families today. We are considerably less concerned with things that happen to someone else, somewhere else; even when, ultimately, they will destroy our way of life

o We expect a technological solution – for more than 300 years technological advances appear to have provided solutions (while actually only creating even more complexity) so we tend to believe that smart people somewhere else are working on the problem

o Our corporatist political structures which seek to balance the views and needs of competing interest groups lack a democratic space for the *public interest*. So, for example, the needs of consumers are balanced against the needs and wishes of banking corporations; the life support needs of citizens are balanced against the profits of the fossil fuel industry; and the urgent need to invest in renewable energy is balanced against the City of London's short term desire to make profits from fracking.

Into this mess, austerity policies can only add further economic instability which will hasten the next financial crash. When it comes, once more the neoclassical economists will claim that "nobody could have seen it coming". More worryingly, once more they will try to blackmail the public into bailing them out. Once again, the instincts of the politicians will be to sacrifice the people in order to bail out the banks. There is an old American saying for this eventuality:

"Fool me once, shame on you. Fool me twice, shame on *me*."

www.ingramcontent.com/pod-product-compliance
Lightning Source LLC
Chambersburg PA
CBHW070841180526
45168CB00002B/916